Extreme

ROCK
CLIMBING

Virginia Loh-Hagan

45th Parallel Press

Published in the United States of America by Cherry Lake Publishing
Ann Arbor, Michigan
www.cherrylakepublishing.com

Content Adviser: John Miller, rock climbing and ice climbing, Michigan
Reading Adviser: Marla Conn, ReadAbility, Inc.
Photo Credits: ©Photobac/Shutterstock.com, cover, 1; ©Photobac/Shutterstock.com, 5; ©Olga Danylenko/Shutterstock.com, 7; ©Photobac/istockphoto.com, 9; ©Oztasbc/istockphoto.com, 11; ©Ingram Publishing/Thinkstock.com, 12; ©Greg Epperson/Shutterstock.com, 15; ©Juanan Barros Moreno/Shutterstock.com, 17; ©Morganamor/Dreamstime.com, 19; ©Vitalii Nesterchuk/Shutterstock.com, 21; ©Greg Epperson/Shutterstock.com, 22; ©Patrick Tehan/TNS/Newscom, 25; ©Greg Epperson/Shutterstock.com, 27; ©Sorokin Donat/ZUMA Press/Newscom, 29; ©Trusjom/Shutterstock.com, multiple interior pages; ©Kues/Shutterstock.com, multiple interior pages

45th Parallel Press is an imprint of Cherry Lake Publishing.

Library of Congress Cataloging-in-Publication Data

Loh-Hagan, Virginia.
  Extreme rock climbing / Virginia Loh-Hagan.
     pages cm. -- (Nailed It!)
  Includes bibliographical references and index.
  ISBN 978-1-63470-020-7 (hardcover) -- ISBN 978-1-63470-074-0 (pdf) -- ISBN 978-1-63470-047-4 (paperback) -- ISBN 978-1-63470-101-3 (ebook)
 1. Rock climbing--Juvenile literature. 2. Extreme sports--Juvenile literature. 3. ESPN X-Games--Juvenile literature. 4. Extreme rock climbing. I. Title.

GV200.2.L595 2015
796.522'3--dc23

                          2015006302

ABOUT THE AUTHOR

Dr. Virginia Loh-Hagan is an author, university professor, former classroom teacher, and curriculum designer. She loves rocks—the kind she can wear on her finger. She lives in San Diego with her very tall husband and very naughty dogs. To learn more about her, visit www.virginialoh.com.

Table of Contents

Doing the Impossible

Why is Lynn Hill a good example of an extreme rock climber? How is rock climbing different from mountaineering? What is El Capitan? What is big wall climbing?

Lynn Hill jams her fingers into small cracks. Her foot slips. Her timing is off. She dangles 2,000 feet (609 meters) above the ground. This is her second time climbing the wall. She failed the first time.

Many people have tried to climb this rock wall. This is where they gave up.

Hill won't quit. She's tired. Her hands are **swollen**, or puffy. She stretches out her arm. She digs in her fingers.

She pushes herself up. She keeps climbing. She climbs for four days. She reaches the top!

Hill did the impossible. She free-climbed the Nose of El Capitan. People said, "No man will ever free the Nose." They were right. A woman did it!

Hill wanted to do better. She returned a year later. She free-climbed the Nose again. She did it in 23 hours. She was daring. Others copied her.

Climbers use cracks in the rock to climb.

Extreme rock climbing is about doing the impossible. It's about **scaling**, or climbing, walls. The challenge is the climbing. It's different from **mountaineering**. Mountaineers hike up mountains. They want to get to the top. Extreme rock climbers want to climb.

NAILED IT!

That Happened?!?

Mitch Parker is an expert rock climber. He lived in a jungle in Belize. Belize is a country in Central America. It is south of Mexico. He was climbing a 200-foot-high (61 m) cliff. He made a wrong move. He threw his rope into a bee hive. He was attacked by Africanized bees. He said, "Within seconds they were covering my head, trying to get in my nose and my mouth." He had to drop down past the hive. He jumped into a stream. He wanted to drown the bees. He was taken to a hospital. Doctors counted more than 150 stings behind one ear. He was stung more than 1,000 times. He recovered three months later.

Scaling steep rock walls challenges rock climbers. Hiking up tall mountains challenges mountaineers.

Climbers like climbing El Capitan. El Capitan means "the captain" in Spanish. It is a rock formation in Yosemite National Park. It is **vertical**. It goes straight up. It is 3,000 feet (914 m) high. The Nose of El Capitan is very hard to climb. It is a really tall cliff.

El Capitan is a "big wall." Big walls are rock **faces**. Faces are surfaces. They have few **holds**. Climbers use holds to pull themselves up. Big walls are 1,000 feet (305 m) or higher. They are steep and vertical. Climbers often sleep on the cliff. They sleep in a hanging tent. Big wall climbing is hard work.

"Big walls are 1,000 feet (305m) or higher."

Climbers like to climb cliffs. Cliffs are steep or overhanging edges of rocks.

Free Falling!

What is free climbing? What is free solo climbing? What are some dangers of free solo climbing?

Lynn Hill is a free climber. Free climbing is a type of extreme rock climbing. Free climbers do not use ropes to climb up. They use ropes to protect themselves. They prepare for falling. Climbers slip all the time. Ropes stop deadly falls.

Free climbers don't get **aid**, or help, from the ropes. They climb using bravery, strength, and chalk dust. Chalk dust keeps hands dry. Their hands rub against the rock. Climbers have strong bodies. They use all their body parts. They use the insides of their feet to climb.

Free climbers depend on their climbing skill. They go really high. Without ropes a fall would be certain injury or death.

Free solo climbing is another type of extreme rock climbing. These climbers don't use ropes at all. They don't use any gear. They only use shoes and a chalk bag.

Alex Honnold is a free solo climber. He climbed El Capitan

Free climbers only use ropes to stop falls.
Aid climbers use ropes to climb up.

Climbers use the same chalk that gymnasts use. Chalk keeps their hands from getting too sweaty.

and two other rock faces. He did it in 18 hours and 50 minutes. He and Cedar Wright biked to 15 mountains. They climbed more than 100,000 (30,480 m) vertical feet. They did this in 22 days.

Mark Bowling climbs in Joshua Tree National Park. He did 200 climbs in 18 hours. He called free solo climbing a "magical feeling."

Extreme Rock Climbing: Know the Lingo

Airtime: long fall

Barndoor: a climber who is holding on by only his left or right hand and foot—he swings out from the wall like a door

Belay: to protect a roped climber from falling by passing the rope through a belay device

Beta: information about a route that helps climbers

Carabiners: metal rings used to guide a climber's safety rope

Deck: the ground

Dyno: jump or leap or lunge

Edging: using the edge of a shoe on a foothold

Greasy: slippery

Gripped: tired or afraid

Pitch: section of a cliff that is climbed between two belay points

Pumped: feeling in the forearms when muscles lose strength after a hard climb

Rappel: descending a rock face by sliding down a rope

Rest: big handholds and footholds that let the climber relax

Send: to cleanly complete a route (short for ascend)

Smearing: when there is no foothold, using the sole of a shoe on the wall

Whip: end of a long fall

Free solo climbing is risky. Derek Hersey climbed in Yosemite. He slipped on a rock. He fell 100 feet (30.5 m). He died.

Deep water soloing is another type of extreme rock climbing. Climbers climb sea cliffs at high tide. The water is at a high level. Climbers fall. The water protects climbers. Small boats pick them up. The water can also be dangerous. Climbers could drown.

Chris Sharma climbed Es Pontas in Spain. It is a natural **arch**, or bridge. It is in water. The wall has few holds. He was upside down. He hung on his arms and fingers. The biggest challenge is a huge jump. In climbing, a jump is called a dyno. Sharma tried to dyno it. He dynoed over 50 times. Climbers don't quit!

"Deep water soloing is another type of extreme rock climbing."

Climbers do all kinds of moves.

Rocking the First Try

Why do climbers need strong minds? What is flash climbing? What is onsight climbing?

Climbers don't waste energy. They can't **panic**, or lose control. They have to stay relaxed. They can't rush to the top. They make one move at a time. They carefully think about their moves. Climbers need to have strong minds.

Climbers like completing **routes** on the first try. Routes are climbing paths.

Flash climbing is when climbers are given some beta. Beta is information. Climbers help each other. They share good holds. They share moves. This helps climbers be successful on their first try.

Onsight climbing is when climbers have no beta. Climbers complete a climb on the first try. They do it without any help. They stand on the ground. They look up. They figure out routes. They look for holds. Onsight climbing is hard.

Ethan Pringle has climbed more than 100 onsights and flashes. He suggests being open to new ideas. Climbers need to make changes as they climb.

Climbers "read the route." They see where they're going by looking up at the rock face.

Adam Ondra has onsighted many difficult climbs. He climbed the hardest route in the Red River **Gorge**. A gorge is a narrow valley. It is between hills or mountains. The rock walls are steep and rocky. Climbers are always looking for routes.

Getting Your Body Ready!

Climbers need to be in good shape. Steph Davis is a free solo climber. She is always working out. She practices climbing on her homemade climbing wall. This is called pulling plastic. She hikes 10 miles (16 km) up mountains. She does this twice a week. She hikes through knee-deep snow. She runs trails. She balances on a slackline. A slackline is a loose tightrope. This is hung high in her yard. Davis wants to be a good climber. She builds her strength and balance.

Routes have cool names. Adam Ondra has onsight climbed "Golden Ticket" and "Pure Imagination."

Unstoppable!

What is redpoint climbing? How is Tommy Caldwell unstoppable?

Some climbers fail to onsight or flash a climb. This means, they didn't finish a climb on the first try. Failing does not stop them. They redpoint the climb instead.

Redpoint climbing is another type of rock climbing. Climbers free-climb a route. They practice the route. They learn about the route.

Tommy Caldwell is one of the best redpoint climbers. He tried seven times to redpoint a wall. The wall is called

Just Do It. This is known as the third hardest climb. It took him three days.

Caldwell is a big wall climber. He free-climbed the Nose. He did it in less than 12 hours.

Not even war stops Caldwell. He and some friends climbed cliffs in Kyrgyzstan. It is a country in central Asia.

The term redpoint comes from Kurt Albert. After he free-climbed a route, he put a red dot at the bottom of the route.

Big wall climbers have to sleep on moveable ledges or hanging tents.

When Extreme Is Too Extreme!

A new form of extreme rock climbing is naked rock climbing. These climbers do not use ropes or safety equipment. They also don't wear clothes. Climbers like the experience of being naked. They say it captures the "true essence of the climbing spirit." They feel closer to nature. Naked rock climbing increases the difficulty level. Being naked means climbers have no protection or safety gear.

There was a war between the government and **rebels**. Rebels are lawbreakers.

Caldwell and his friends camped out. They used **ledges**, or shelves, on the mountain. They used tents. They were hundreds of feet in the air.

They heard gunshots. They were captured by rebels. They were prisoners for six days. One day, they were alone with a **captor**. A captor is a kidnapper.

Caldwell pushed him over the edge. They saw him fall. They used their climbing skills. They climbed for several miles. They found an army camp. They were safe. Caldwell learned that the captor survived the fall. But he was then sentenced to death.

Caldwell doesn't let accidents stop him. He injured his finger. He couldn't use it to climb. So he had part of the finger removed. He climbs with nine fingers.

Caldwell and Kevin Jorgeson free-climbed the Dawn Wall. It is part of El Capitan. It is the steepest and tallest section. It catches the morning sun. So it gets hot. They were the first to free climb it. They've tried to free climb this wall several times. They practiced for five years. They lived on the wall. They fell many times. Their fingers had painful

Tommy Caldwell and Kevin Jorgeson started free-climbing the Dawn Wall on December 27, 2014. They finished on January 14, 2015.

cuts. They rested. They waited for their skin to heal. They taped and glued their cuts. Jorgeson said, "I'm not giving up. I will rest. I will try again. I will succeed."

This climb was thought to be impossible. Free climbers do impossible things. They are unstoppable.

Beyond Mountains

Why is extreme rock climbing dangerous? What is bouldering? What are other variations of rock climbing?

Extreme rock climbing is dangerous. Loose rocks are dangerous. Sudden weather changes are dangerous. Climbers can fall. They can break body parts. Falling rocks can hit them. Climbers need to be smart. They use their skills. They are creative.

Climbers need the right gear. Jimmy Jewell climbed in sneakers. He slipped and fell. He died. Climbers have to wear special shoes. The shoe bottoms are sticky rubber.

Climbers don't need high, huge walls to be extreme.

Bouldering is climbing on **boulders**. Boulders are large rocks. They're no higher than 20 feet (6 m). They are smaller than mountains. It's safer to jump off boulders. Bouldering can be done without gear. Climbers can safely practice difficult and new moves. They use foam pads. They land on them if they fall.

Alain Robert is an **urban**, or city, climber. He free solo climbs **skyscrapers**, or tall buildings. He grips his feet and knees against the wall. He has **vertigo**. This means he gets dizzy. But this doesn't stop him.

There is nothing more extreme than dangling off the face of a mountain.

Phil Shaw invented "extreme ironing." He had laundry to iron. He wanted to rock climb instead. So he ironed while rock climbing. A friend carried a board on his back. About 1,500 people do this.

NAILED IT!

Spotlight Biography: Ashima Shiraishi

Ashima Shiraishi climbs boulders. At 10 years old, she climbed the Crown of Aragorn. It juts out at a 45-degree angle. This is a really hard route. Climbers need to twist their bodies. They need to hang upside down by their fingers. Only a few female climbers can climb this rock. Shiraishi is the best U.S. climber in her age group. She's "sending problems," or climbing routes, that most adults can't do. She started climbing at age 2. Her parents saw her climbing Rat Rock in Central Park in New York. Rat Rock is a boulder. It is 15 feet (4.5 m) high and 40 feet (12 m) wide. Her father is her coach. He's a modern dancer. He said, "With dance, there is space all around you. I teach her to think about the space around her when she is climbing."

Alain Robert is known as the "Human Spider."

There are many benefits of rock climbing. Climbing builds muscle. It boosts brainpower. It builds problem-solving skills. In bouldering, a route is called a problem. Climbers solve problems. They figure out how to climb.

Cedar Wright said, "Climbing is an amazing teacher, instilling focus, balance, determination, and … valuable life skills."

Did You Know?

- Climbers go to the bathroom wherever they can. This means they go in nature. They stay away from plants, climbing routes, streams, and trails. They get rid of their own waste. They carry plastic bags for used toilet paper. While big wall climbing, climbers have to do their business. They pee in the air. They use toilet sacks, called "wag bags." They save these to trash later. Or they send the bags to helpers on the ground.

- Climbers like to name climbs. Jose Pereyra was a free climber. He created a route in southern Utah. It's a 100-foot (30.5 m) climb. He named it "No Way, Jose!"

- Climbers play a game called Add On. One climber does a route. The next climber repeats the route and adds a move. This is repeated until they get bored or tired.

- Rock climbers have nicknames. They are called rock hounds, rock jocks, or wall rats.

- Climbers wear shoes that are a size or two smaller than their normal shoes. They also don't wear socks. They want to have a tight fit. They want to feel the rock.

- Climbers' hands can get really ugly. Sometimes, climbers get flappers. A flapper is when a rough patch of skin separates from the hand. This happens while climbing. The skin rips off all at once. It looks like a big flap.

Consider This!

TAKE A POSITION! Some people think rock climbing should be part of the Olympics. Adam Ondra said, "I think climbing deserves to be an Olympic sport, as it is one of the few natural movements—like swimming or running—that is not part of the Olympics." Other climbers do not agree. They would rather win personal goals than gold medals. Should rock climbing be an Olympic sport? Argue your point with reasons and evidence.

SAY WHAT? Extreme rock climbers use many of the same skills as mountaineers. Mountaineers climb to explore. But rock climbers are also different from mountaineers. Learn more about mountaineering. Explain the differences and similarities between the two sports.

THINK ABOUT IT! Rock climbing has a grading system. This system describes the difficulty and danger of climbing the route. There are five classes. Class 1 describes easy hikes. Class 5 is where a fall may result in death. Compare this grading system to your grading system at school. Why do we need grades?

SEE A DIFFERENT SIDE! The U.S. Forest Service bans some climbing gear. Climbing gear could become a permanent part of the rock formation. Bouldering causes concerns as well. Officials worry about destroying nature. Many climbers believe in "leave no trace" and "minimal impact." This means they leave nature as they found it. How can rock climbing be harmful to nature?

Learn More: Resources

PRIMARY SOURCES

McNamara, Chris. *How to Big Wall Climb*. Mill Valley, CA: SuperTopo, 2012, www.supertopo.com/topos/htbw-free.pdf

Vertical Frontier: *A History of the Art, Sport, and Philosophy of Rock Climbing in Yosemite*, a documentary (2002).

SECONDARY SOURCES

Roberts, Jeremy. *Rock and Ice Climbing: Top the Tower*. New York: Rosen Central, 2000.

Ryan, Pat. *Rock Climbing*. Mankato, MN: Smart Apple Media, 2000.

Takeda, Pete. *Climb! Your Guide to Bouldering, Sport Climbing, Trad Climbing, Ice Climbing, Alpinism and More*. Turtleback Books, 2002.

WEB SITES

International Climbing and Mountaineering Federation: http://theuiaa.org

International Federation of Sport Climbing: www.ifsc-climbing.org

Glossary

aid (AYD) help, using equipment or gear

arch (AHRCH) bridge

boulders (BOHL-durz) large rocks

captor (KAP-tor) kidnapper

faces (FA-sez) rock surfaces

gorge (GORJ) narrow valley between hills or mountains with steep, rocky walls

holds (HOLDZ) cracks, ledges, and other features climbers use

ledge (LEJ) shelf on the mountain walls

mountaineering (moun-tuhn-EER-ing) a sport in which people hike up mountains

panic (PAN-ik) losing control due to fear

rebels (REB-uhlz) people who go against the government in charge

routes (ROUTS) climbing paths

scaling (SKALE-ing) climbing a steep wall

skyscrapers (SKYE-skray-purz) tall buildings in a busy city

swollen (SWOH-luhn) puffy

urban (UR-buhn) city

vertical (VUR-ti-kuhl) straight up

vertigo (VUR-ti-go) a condition when people get dizzy

Index